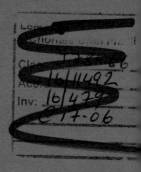

Forming a band

Richard Spilsbury

Raintree is an imprint of Capstone Global Library Limited, a company incorporated in England and Wales having its registered office at 7 Pilgrim Street, London, EC4V 6LB – Registered company number: 6695582

www.raintreepublishers.co.uk
myorders@raintreepublishers.co.uk

Edited by Clare Lewis, Mandy Robbins, Penny West and James Benefield
Designed by Steve Mead
Original illustrations © Capstone Global Library Ltd 2015
Picture research by Ruth Blair and Tracy Cummins
Production by Victoria Fitzgerald
Originated by Capstone Global Library Ltd
Printed and bound in China by CTPS

ISBN 978 1 406 28248 1 (hardback)
18 17 16 15 14
10 9 8 7 6 5 4 3 2 1

British Library Cataloguing in Publication Data
A full catalogue record for this book is available from the British Library.

Acknowledgements
We would like to thank the following for permission to reproduce photographs: Corbis pp. 22 (© Troy House), 36 (© Ocean), 38 (© Nicole Hill/Rubberball); Getty Images pp. 5 (Theo Wargo/Wirelmage), 6 (Neil Beckerman), 7 (Yellow Dog Productions), 8 (Gary S Chapman), 9 (Digital Vision), 11 bottom (Samir Hussein/Redferns), 11 top (Popperfoto), 13 (Redferns), 16 (Ian Gavan), 18 (Micky Simawi/Photoshot), 19 (Richard McLean), 21 (Joey Foley), 23 (Pascal Broze), 26 (Heidi Gutman/NBC NewsWire), 27 bottom right (Gary Miller/FilmMagic), 27 bottom left (Jeff Kravitz/FilmMagic), 27 top (Jim Dyson), 28 (Sergio del Grande/Mondadori Portfolio), 30 (Kevin Mazur/Wirelmage), 31 (Christie Goodwin), 32, 33 (Image Source), 35 (David Livingston), 39 (Oleg Prikhodko); Shutterstock pp. 4 (Ilike), 14 (pmdc2952), 15 bottom left (Venus Ange), 15 middle left (Elena Schweitzer), 15 top right (Sideways Design), 17 bottom left (dean bertoncelj), 17 bottom right (Mike Flippo), 17 top (Keith Publicover), 25 (Clive Chilvers), 37 (HomeStudio), 24 (Findlay Rankin / age footstock).

Artistic Effects: Shutterstock.

Cover photograph reproduced with permission of Corbis (© Michelle Pedone).

We would like to thank Matt Anniss for his invaluable help in the preparation of this book.

CONTENTS

SO, YOU WANT TO FORM A BAND?

So, you want to form a band? That's great. Being in a band means you get to spend even more time listening to and playing your favourite kind of music. And you will be able to do so with bandmates who share the same interests as you.

Forming a band seems like an easy thing to do, because lots of new bands form every day. But most of these bands fall apart after a few months, never practise enough to become great, or spend more time worrying about how they look than how they sound. So how do you put together a band that's actually going to be any good?

That is where this book comes in. Read on to find out how to find bandmates, choose gear, plan rehearsals and keep the band together. Forming a band is not easy, but it might be one of the best things you ever do!

BEING IN A BAND WILL GIVE YOU THE CHANCE TO SHARE YOUR LOVE OF MUSIC WITH OTHERS.

I really loved music, and I had to do something about it. It started out as just playing acoustic Weezer songs in my bedroom, but quickly I got the band together, and even though Johnny had never played bass in his life, it clicked on the very first day. Now we're about to hop in a van and drive to Berlin. I still find it amazing.

Dougy Mandagi of Australian indie rock band The Temper Trap

Did you know?

Some of the biggest bands in the history of music formed at school or university. These include U2, the Beatles, Green Day and Genesis.

KELLY ROWLAND, BEYONCÉ KNOWLES AND MICHELLE WILLIAMS MADE UP DESTINY'S CHILD.

WHY START A BAND?

The two most important reasons for starting a band are a love of music and wanting to play with other musicians.

For love, not money

Lots of people decide to start a band because they want to be rich and famous. Big mistake! A few bands achieve this, but most never get anywhere close to fame or fortune. If they are lucky, they have fun playing around the area they live in, bringing pleasure to friends and local fans of live music. If making money is your aim, you might be disappointed!

The reality is that it usually *costs* people money to be in a band because there are so many expenses. Many bands get paid so little for gigs that the fee barely covers the expenses. So, start a band to share your love of music with others, such as the people who listen to your songs or turn up to your gigs.

START A BAND FOR THE LOVE OF MUSIC, NOT FOR FAME AND FORTUNE!

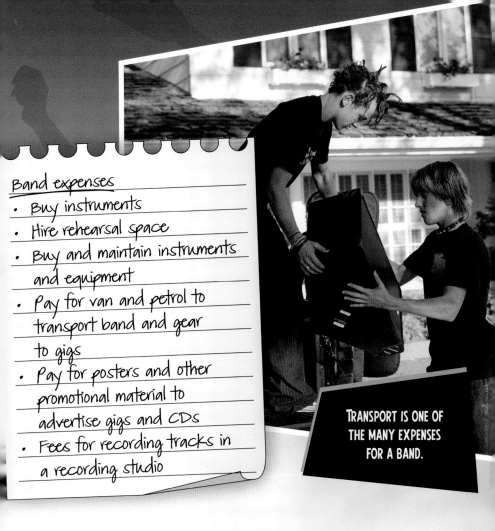

Band expenses

- Buy instruments
- Hire rehearsal space
- Buy and maintain instruments and equipment
- Pay for van and petrol to transport band and gear to gigs
- Pay for posters and other promotional material to advertise gigs and CDs
- Fees for recording tracks in a recording studio

TRANSPORT IS ONE OF THE MANY EXPENSES FOR A BAND.

BANDSPEAK

roadie a member of technical support staff or crew. Roadies help to stage music concerts and other events. They set up before a gig, look after the instruments during the show and pack away afterwards. Most bands that are just starting up will not have roadies ... they do the hard work themselves!

It is good for you!

Being in a band is good for you. Not good for you in the same way as eating your vegetables or taking regular exercise! Good for you because it makes you more motivated, boosts your confidence and brings you new friends!

BEING IN A BAND MAKES YOU PRACTISE!

It makes you better!

Playing in a band makes you a better musician. It is more fun to practise with others. You will focus on your music more because you do not want to let your bandmates down. There is nothing like an upcoming gig in front of a hall full of schoolmates. It makes you work hard at learning those tricky scales and chords once and for all!

It makes you strong

We are not talking bulging biceps here. We are talking strength of character. Once you have missed a cue or played a wrong note in front of a crowd, you soon learn to get over it fast, make a joke of it and play on. Being in a band teaches you to bounce back from problems rather than let problems bring you down.

It makes you friends

Sharing music is a buzz. When you play a song with your band and it sounds good, it is a great feeling. Working together can help members of a band become long-lasting friends, whether or not the band stays together.

IT IS FUN PLAYING SONGS FOR YOUR OWN ENJOYMENT, BUT IT IS EVEN BETTER TO SHARE YOUR MUSIC WITH OTHERS.

BANDSPEAK

scale set of notes sung in order going up or down in pitch (highness or lowness).

chord combination of three or more notes of a scale that blend harmoniously when played together.

INSPIRED

ROLLING WITH THE STONES

The Rolling Stones are the longest performing rock and roll band of all time. Many of their famous hits like "(I Can't Get No) Satisfaction", which first made it big back in 1965, are still played all over the world. The two founding members met at school in the early 1950s, and singer Mick Jagger, guitarist Keith Richards and drummer Charlie Watts are still bandmates today!

In the early 1950s, Keith Richards and Mick Jagger were classmates at primary school, until Jagger went to a different school. Nearly 10 years later, in 1960, the pair met by chance at a train station in London. After chatting for a while, they soon realized they were both into music. Jagger had been singing in clubs, while Richards had been playing guitar since he was 14. They once again became friends and in 1962 they formed a band along with drummer Charlie Watts and others. The band was named after the track Rollin Stone by American blues musician Muddy Waters.

Rolling Stones output	
Studio albums	29
Live albums	18
Compilation albums	33
Singles	109
Video albums	20
Music videos	57
Box sets	5

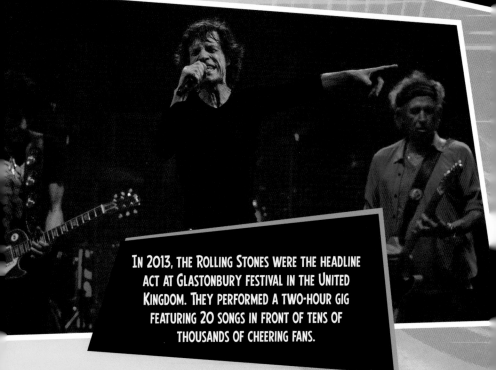

It was the song that really made The Rolling Stones, changed us from just another band into a huge, monster band.

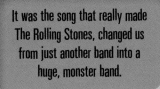

Mick Jagger talking about the song "(I Can't Get No) Satisfaction"

THIS PHOTO WAS TAKEN IN 1963 WHEN THE ROLLING STONES WERE JUST STARTING OUT.

IN 2013, THE ROLLING STONES WERE THE HEADLINE ACT AT GLASTONBURY FESTIVAL IN THE UNITED KINGDOM. THEY PERFORMED A TWO-HOUR GIG FEATURING 20 SONGS IN FRONT OF TENS OF THOUSANDS OF CHEERING FANS.

WHAT WILL YOU PLAY?

Before you form a band you need to know what instrument you are going to play. How do you choose the instrument that is right for you? What is the best way to get hold of one without breaking the bank?

Listen up!

The best way to choose which instrument to play is by gut instinct. What grabs you when you are choosing music to download or listening to tunes on a friend's MP3 player? Do you find yourself strumming an invisible guitar or beating the table with your fingers in time to the drums? Or maybe it is the higher pitches of a flute that sings to you? The instrument that appeals to you most is probably the one you should play.

BANDSPEAK

pitch describes the highness or lowness of a sound. A tuba has a lower pitched sound than a flute, for example.

Keep it real

Of course, you still need to be practical, too. Choose an instrument that suits your size. If you are small, then a flute is obviously much lighter, smaller and easier to hold and carry to band practice than a huge double bass. You might also have to consult your folks! If they think drums will be too loud for the neighbours, you might have to think again.

Band Tech: DIGITAL DRUMS

Some drummers choose digital drums that you can listen to through headphones for silent practice.

The pads are laid out on a stand like an acoustic drum kit.

The pads have sensors that generate electric signals when hit, that in turn produce drum sounds.

Digital drums often have useful features such as a metronome and play-along songs.

Sound and rhythm

Another thing to consider is the way different instruments make sounds. To make music, you pluck, blow or hit instruments in different ways. What appeals to you most?

Good vibrations

Musicians pluck a guitar string or hit a drum to make it vibrate. This makes the air around the instruments vibrate, too. These vibrations spread outwards as sound waves that we hear as sounds when they enter our ears. Different instruments make different sounds depending on what is vibrating (for example, a string or drum skin), how it is played (plucked, hit or blown) and the shape and size of the instrument.

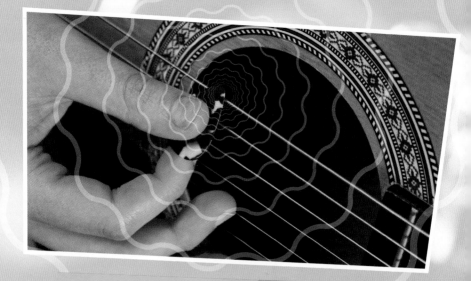

Strange though it sounds, the piano is a stringed instrument! When we press piano keys, soft hammers hit strings inside the instrument. Then the strings vibrate to play notes.

Did you Know?

Band Tech: Different Instruments

Trumpets, trombones and other brass instruments are mostly made of brass or another metal. You play them by buzzing your lips against the mouthpiece. This makes air vibrate inside the instrument to produce notes.

Drums, cymbals, triangles, timpani, xylophones and other percussion instruments usually make sounds when you hit them with a stick, mallet or your hand. Some percussion instruments, such as the xylophone, are pitched to play different notes or sounds.

You can pluck or strum some stringed instruments and rub a bow across others, like the violin. Bigger instruments, such as cellos and double basses, generally sound deeper or lower than smaller ones, such as violins and guitars.

You blow into a woodwind instrument to vibrate

air inside it. Sound is made by blowing over the top of an opening (the flute) or by blowing into a reed (a clarinet or saxophone). Big horns, such as the baritone sax, make deeper sounds.

Try before you buy

It is best to try out your chosen instrument before you buy it. That way, you will not waste your savings or your parents' hard-earned cash! Ask around – you might be able to borrow an instrument from relations, friends or neighbours. Ask local schools or music tutors where to hire an instrument. Join a school band or orchestra so you can try out their instruments. If you do decide to buy, you could go for a good beginner model or second-hand equipment.

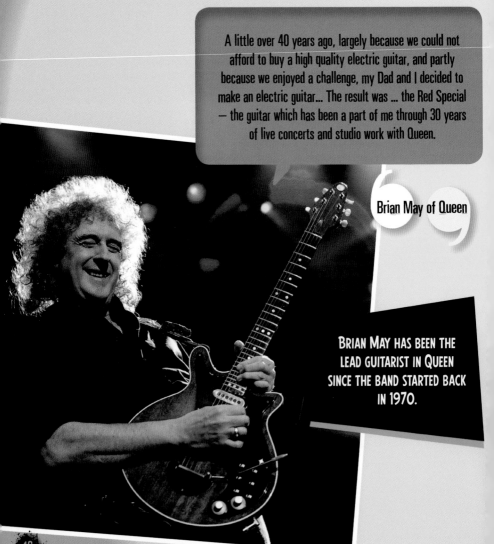

A little over 40 years ago, largely because we could not afford to buy a high quality electric guitar, and partly because we enjoyed a challenge, my Dad and I decided to make an electric guitar... The result was ... the Red Special – the guitar which has been a part of me through 30 years of live concerts and studio work with Queen.

Brian May of Queen

BRIAN MAY HAS BEEN THE LEAD GUITARIST IN QUEEN SINCE THE BAND STARTED BACK IN 1970.

BaND TeCH: KNOW YOUR GUITaRS

Trying out instruments before you buy gives you the chance to find exactly the right one for you. After all, there are so many options – even if you know you really want to play the guitar!

A regular acoustic guitar has six strings that each make a different note when you pluck or strum them. The strings vibrate to make a certain sound and the hollow shape of the guitar body makes those sounds louder.

A bass guitar has just the lowest four strings of a normal six-string guitar. A bass guitarist plays patterns of low notes. These accompany tunes with higher notes played on other instruments.

Electric guitars have thin metal strings with pickups underneath. These turn a string's vibration into an electrical signal. The signals travel through an amplifier that changes them into much louder sounds.

Mix it up!

Another good reason to borrow or rent an instrument is that it gives you time to make sure that it's the one for you. If you realize it is not, you can still pick another instrument. It is also good to learn more than one instrument when forming a band. Lots of bands today have songs in their sets in which they swap instruments to play the song.

Did you Know?

When Flea (real name Michael Peter Balzary) was young he was into jazz and learned to play the trumpet. As a teenager he got into rock so he took up bass guitar. More recently he learned to play the piano, too! Now he plays all three instruments in his band the Red Hot Chili Peppers.

Don't forget the extras

When you do buy an instrument, or persuade your family to get you one for a gift, do not forget the extras. There are things you need for your instrument. You might need a case to carry it in, a music stand to hold your music, and for instruments like the sax, sets of new reeds.

Electric guitar extras
- Plectrum to pluck the strings
- Case to carry the guitar in
- Strap to support guitar while you play
- Amplifier
- Tuner

Looking after your gear

This may not sound very rock and roll, but good musicians look after their instruments. Buy proper cases for your instruments and use them. Take that extra minute to put them away after practice. Don't leave them leaning against the bed where the dog might knock them over. If you look after your instrument it will last and save you money in the long run.

TAKING CARE OF INSTRUMENTS MEANS THEY LAST LONGER AND PLAY BETTER.

GET IT TOGETHER

So, you have chosen your instrument and you want to form a band, but how do you meet other musicians? And when you meet them, how will you know which singer or player to choose? Read on ... the answers you need are all here!

Spread the word

The people you need for your band could be anywhere around you, so spread the word. Tell everyone you know that you are starting a band and what kind of music you want to play. Talk to classmates, family, friends and friends-of-friends. Ask music teachers and tutors who they know. Find out who else in your school plays musical instruments. You could put up posters at school or clubs you go to, asking interested musicians to put forward their names.

Put yourself out there

Don't wait for things to happen. Join music clubs, go to auditions for music shows at school and in the community. Join marching bands or school orchestras. Doing these things will help improve your musical skills and knowledge and you will meet lots of other musicians. Some might be itching to join a band just like yours!

Destiny's Child began when eight-year-old Beyoncé Knowles met LaTavia Roberson while auditioning for a kids singing group in Houston, Texas, USA.

TALENT SHOWS ARE A GOOD PLACE TO MEET SINGERS AND MUSICIANS.

If you make contact with other musicians via the Internet, remember cybersafety rules. It is not a good idea to meet people you have only communicated with online, because you could put yourself at risk. Only ever do so in a public place when you are with parents or other adults.

Who's got talent?

If you're lucky, you will end up finding several musicians and singers who would like to join your band. Now you have to work out who you should choose.

Hold auditions

You could hold an audition. This gives you the chance to hear all the musicians play. You could even ask them all to learn to play the same song, to make it easier to compare them. Find somewhere to hold the audition. Make a poster telling people where and when it will be held and what type of music to play. Make sure your advert is persuasive, too!

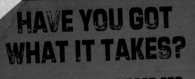

HAVE YOU GOT WHAT IT TAKES?

GUITARIST SEEKS SINGER AND MUSICIANS TO FORM A GREAT NEW ROCK BAND.

AUDITIONS IN THE HALL, WEDNESDAY 6TH AUGUST AT 4.15

INVITE SOMEONE YOU TRUST TO COME ALONG TO THE AUDITIONS TO HELP YOU CHOOSE NEW BANDMATES.

Best for the band

A word of warning. Don't choose bandmates on skill alone. You will be spending a lot of time with these people, so you need to get along. If someone plays or sings brilliantly, but starts arguments the minute he or she enters the room, let them walk. You need people who play well, but who are also easy-going and happy to work as a team.

JUST BECAUSE SOMEONE IS A GREAT MUSICIAN DOES NOT MEAN THEY ARE THE BEST CHOICE FOR YOUR BAND...

Checklist for band members:
- ✓ A musician who enjoys playing the same music style as the rest of the band.
- ✓ A musician who is on roughly the same level of skill as the rest of the band.
- ✓ A musician who is a similar age to you, is keen and will turn up for rehearsals.

Pick and choose

When you are choosing a line-up it is good to keep your options open. A typical band has four members: a guitarist, a drummer, a bass player and a singer. Lots of bands choose not to stick to this formula, though!

The basic set-up for a band works because the lead guitarist plays the tune or melody, the drummer creates the main rhythm, the bass guitarist plays the background rhythms and chords and the singer sings the lyrics (words to the song). But you can have any instruments and different mixes of instruments you like, such as two bass players, a violinist, a saxophonist or a DJ on a computer.

BANDSPEAK

rhythm strong, regular, repeated pattern of sound.

A VIOLIN IS AN UNUSUAL CHOICE FOR A BAND. MAYBE IT COULD WORK FOR YOU, THOUGH!

The choice of instruments in your band line-up also depends on the type of music you play. Typical instruments found in a reggae band include bass, drums, guitar, organ and melodica (musical keyboard on top, played by blowing air through a mouthpiece in the side). And it probably goes without saying that a steel drum band is made up of many drum players!

STEEL DRUM BANDS CONSIST OF ONLY DRUMS. BUT SOME OTHER BANDS USE STEEL PANS IN THEIR LINE-UP, TOO.

I wanted to do something that was a bit more idiosyncratic, hence the switch to another instrument. When Jethro Tull began, I think I'd been playing the flute for about two weeks. It was a quick learning curve... literally every night I walked onstage was a flute lesson.

Ian Anderson, vocalist, flautist and acoustic guitarist of British rock band Jethro Tull

INSPIRED

BREAKING THE MOULD!

Your band can have any variety of instruments and players – it is not all about guitars and drums! There are lots of examples of rock bands that use a variety of instruments, such as saxophone, flute, clarinet, French horn and trumpet. Here are just a few...

E STREET BAND

TYPE OF MUSIC: Rock

ORIGINATED: USA

YEARS ACTIVE: 1972 to 1989, 1995, 1999 to the present

LINE-UP: Bruce Springsteen (lead vocals, guitar, harmonica, piano, synthesizer, glockenspiel), Steven van Zandt (guitar, mandolin), Roy Bittan (piano, keyboards, accordion, vocals), Max Weinberg (drums), Nils Lofgren (guitar, slide guitar, accordion, backing vocals), Patti Scialfa (vocals, guitar)

NICK CAVE AND THE BAD SEEDS

Type of music: Alternative rock

Originated: Australia

Years active: 1983 to the present

Line-up: Nick Cave (vocals, piano, organ, harmonica, percussion, electric guitar, string arrangements), Thomas Wydler (drums, percussion, vocals), Martyn P. Casey (bass, vocals), Conway Savage (piano, organ, vocals), Jim Sclavunos (percussion, drums, organ, melodica, vocals), Warren Ellis (violin, Fender Mandocaster, loops, mandolin, tenor guitar, viola, bouzouki, accordion, flute, lute, piano, programming, percussion, string arrangements, vocals)

Arcade Fire

Type of music: Indie rock

Originated: Canada

Years active: c. 2001 to the present

Instruments: guitar, drums, bass guitar, piano, violin, viola, cello, double bass, xylophone, glockenspiel, keyboard, French horn, accordion, harp, mandolin, and hurdy-gurdy

DIXIE CHICKS

Type of music: Country, pop

Originated: USA

Years active: 1989 to the present

Line-up: Natalie Maines (vocals, guitar, bass), Emily Robinson (banjo, guitar, bass, mandolin, accordion, sitar), Martie Maguire (violin, viola, acoustic guitar, double bass, mandolin)

Bands are at their best when musicians have fun playing music together and working as a team. When band members are tense or upset with each other, the music can suffer.

making

Working as a team

Forming a band should be a team effort. Not everyone can be lead singer or lead guitarist. The musician best suited to the job should do it. That might mean some people have to take on a different role from the one they hoped for. Paul McCartney started out as a guitarist. He switched to bass when the band lost their original bass player, but he and the rest of the Beatles did okay!

So it was like, uh-oh, we haven't got a bass player. And everyone sort of turned round and looked at me. I was a bit lumbered with it, really — it was like, "Well ... it'd better be you, then."

Paul McCartney of the Beatles on the moment he became the bass player

it work

Taking the lead

It is sensible to choose one person to be the band leader or spokesperson. The leader does not have to be the one who thought of forming the band. It should be the person who is good at making decisions. The leader arranges rehearsals, organizes venues, keeps a diary of dates for rehearsals and gigs, and takes responsibility for contacting the rest of the band if a date changes.

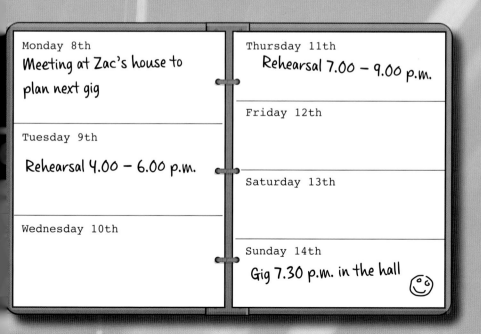

Monday 8th
Meeting at Zac's house to plan next gig

Tuesday 9th
Rehearsal 4.00 – 6.00 p.m.

Wednesday 10th

Thursday 11th
Rehearsal 7.00 – 9.00 p.m.

Friday 12th

Saturday 13th

Sunday 14th
Gig 7.30 p.m. in the hall

Choosing a name

Now you have got a band together, you need to choose a band name. This is important. If you don't think this through, you could end up with an embarrassingly awful name that might put people off your music!

The entire band usually chooses a name together. You could pick a name that you all like the sound of, or that means something to you all. If you get stuck, each band member could suggest four adjectives and four nouns. Then make a band name using one of each! Once you have a name, check on the internet that it is not already being used.

LADY GAGA'S NAME COMES FROM ONE OF HER FAVOURITE SONGS, "RADIO GAGA" BY THE BAND QUEEN.

✓ DO

✓ Choose an unusual name that will come up quickly in an internet search.

✓ Choose a name that is short and easy to read and spell, so it is easy to remember.

✓ Choose a name that matches the music you make. If you play cheery pop, choose a cheery sounding name.

✗ DON'T

✗ Choose too silly or funny a name. The joke will get old really fast.

✗ Use special symbols that are hard to search for on the internet and hard to say.

✗ Try to be too cool or current as this could soon sound old-fashioned.

THE LINKIN PARK LINE-UP.

Did you know?

Linkin Park's original name was already used by another band. Lead singer Chester Bennington came up with a new name when driving past Lincoln Park in California. However, the band changed the spelling to Linkin Park. Buying the web site address from the government might have been difficult!

Getting on

There are endless stories in the news about bands that break up because their members do not get on. You can take steps to avoid this. You will need to work together to solve any problems if you want to stay together.

Delight in disagreements

There are lots of decisions in a band that can cause disagreements, such as what songs to perform and how to play them. Disagreements are perfectly normal and can be a good thing. When people disagree and talk through an issue together without getting into an argument, they often come up with a new, better way of doing things. This could be an improved version of a song or a better way of playing it.

U2 nearly broke up while recording the album *Achtung Baby* in 1991, because of disagreements over the direction of the band's sound. Then guitarist The Edge played a riff that brought the band together. It was for the song "One". "One" is a ballad about the struggle to keep a troubled relationship together!

Did you know?

Communication and compromise

Communication is vital! All band members need to feel like they can contribute and that they will be listened to. So, make sure everyone gets a chance to give their opinions and that everyone else in the band listens to them when they do. Try to see each other's point of view and to work out a way of compromising – coming to a decision that everyone can live with.

BANDS NEED HARMONY IN THEIR PERSONAL RELATIONSHIPS AS WELL AS HARMONY IN THEIR MUSIC!

READY TO ROCK

Now that you have selected an instrument (or instruments) and found some band members, it is time to get to work. That means practising on your own at home and meeting together as a band for some serious rehearsal sessions.

Rehearsals

Every band has to rehearse. Rehearsing is a chance for your band to practise songs together and get to know each other better. You will only play together well and nail those harmonies if you rehearse a lot. Agree on a time and date and make sure everyone in the band turns up. If you rehearse properly, you will know what works and what does not.

Practising can be fun, but it's also serious business. The same goes for band rehearsals. Sure, it's great to hang out and be a part of the gang, but the fact is, rehearsals are about getting stuff done.

Joe Satriani, rock guitarist

Work it out!

If a band member has an off day and has trouble playing a song, it can be frustrating for the others to have to keep playing it again and again. Instead of blaming that person for not practising enough, it can help to just move on to something else and return to the tricky song later. If everyone can be considerate of each other's feelings, rehearsals will be a lot more productive!

BandSpeak

harmonies notes that are played or sung together in a particular way to make a pleasing sound.

Joe's Garage

Rock legend Frank Zappa once penned an entire rock opera dedicated to a struggling teenager and his first attempts to play in a rock and roll band. It was called, fittingly, *Joe's Garage*. The setting for the story was ideal, because almost every successful musician spent time playing music in someone's garage when they were first starting out.

Garages – or spaces like them – are perfect places for young musicians to rehearse in. They are usually big enough to fit all your instruments and if you are lucky, to store them. Another important factor is that a garage is free – so long as you can convince your parents (or someone else's parents) to let you use it!

Possible practice spaces
- Garage
- Cellar
- Bedroom
- Shed
- Village or school hall

HOW ABOUT USING A FAMILY OR FRIEND'S GARAGE TO REHEARSE IN?

Sound matters

If the space you use for rehearsals is close to neighbours, you might need to soundproof it. Soundproofing means adding surfaces to walls and ceilings that will absorb the sound instead of allowing it to bounce off. This reduces the amount of sound passing in and out of the room. Real soundproofing is expensive, so improvise with free stuff such as egg boxes!

SOUNDPROOFING DOS AND DON'TS

✓ DO

- ✓ Fix used carpet to the walls and ceiling. This is free if someone is chucking it out.
- ✓ Use old fabric furniture pads being dumped by local furniture stores and moving companies.
- ✓ Use heavy fabric curtains and put blankets over doors and windows.
- ✓ Put thick rugs over wooden floors.

✗ DON'T

- ✗ Put soundproofing too close to lights as it can catch on fire.
- ✗ Put soundproofing over electrical sockets.

Get to it!

You have got your bandmates and your gear together and you have practised until you are out of breath and your fingers are sore. Now it is time to get in front of an audience and show them what you have got!

Play wherever you can. Pick up the phone, tell all your friends, ask around. Play for free and play for fun. Practice is the only way to get better and better and become super confident when playing together in front of audiences.

Places to play
- School assemblies
- Talent shows
- Fundraisers
- "Open mic" nights
- Youth clubs
- Youth festivals

Or maybe you prefer to be a studio mastermind, cranking out tunes with your band and recording them on a digital recorder. It is totally up to you. Just don't give up. It is a long road ahead and along the way you will have setbacks. You will probably hear the word "no" a lot! Just don't let the problems drag you down. Focus on the buzz you get from playing music with other people and you will stay happy and keep going. Good luck!

Headline acts

Many bands have members who met as young musicians and continued on to great success over many years. Could your band join this headline list in the future?

Take That	1990–1996, 2005–present
Muse	1994–present
The Who	1964–present (with several breaks in between!)
Rush	1968–present
TLC	1991–2003, 2008–present
The Supremes	1959–1977

AS WE HAVE SEEN, BEING IN A BAND CAN TAKE YOU MANY PLACES AND, POSSIBLY BEST OF ALL, SET YOU UP WITH FRIENDS FOR LIFE.

From backroom to the bigtime!

Decide why you want to form a band

Try out different instruments

Choose an instrument

Advertise for band members

Hold auditions

Choose your bandmates

Find venues and start doing gigs

Rehearse

Find a practice space

Choose a name

Organize band meetings

Choose a leader

Decide on the final band line-up

QUIZ

What if you love several kinds of music and you are unsure what style of band you want to form? Take this quiz to find out which style to try first. It is a bit of fun and it might help you get things started!

1 When you go out what do you like to wear?
a) Clothes in the latest fashion
b) Ripped jeans and T-shirt
c) Hoodie, sunglasses, maybe a baseball cap
d) All black

2 Which of these band names do you like best?
a) The Superstars
b) Smash the System
c) Dub Crew
d) Mad Metal

3 What type of songs do you like best?
a) Love songs
b) Songs that fight the power
c) Songs that express what real life is like on the street
d) I don't listen to the words – I just want to rock this place!

4 What stage name would you prefer?
a) Your own name
b) Chaos
c) DJ Bigg
d) Shredder

5 Which of these album names appeals to you most?
a) *Baby, You're Breaking my Heart*
b) *Down with Authority*
c) *Life on the Street*
d) *Hear the Noize!*

6 What kind of vocal style do you like?
a) Melodic singing
b) Fast and angry
c) Clear and spoken more than sung
d) Loud and wild

7 Would people put you on their easy listening playlist?
a) Yes, absolutely
b) Never
c) Maybe
d) We don't "do" easy listening music...

8 What would you like to do on stage?
a) Some great dance routines
b) Jump around and head bang
c) Focus on the lyrics
d) Thrash out some distorted electric guitar riffs

9 Which of these things would people expect to see at one of your concerts?
a) Cool, stylish costumes
b) Sweat and screaming
c) Lots of people bobbing their heads to the beat
d) A shirtless lead singer

10 Which of these lyrics sound most like something your band would sing?
a) "Tonight, we'll be together again, baby, oh yeahhh."
b) "It's time to take the power back/ To get the government back on track."
c) "I'm taking one for the team/ Living the dream/ Or least that's how it seems..."
d) "He came from the edge of town/ Had a heart of stone..."

Answers

IF YOU ANSWERED MOSTLY AS: You show all the signs of becoming a pop megastar! You will probably enjoy making pop music that people can dance to, singing love songs with simple rhythms and harmonies, and lighting up the stage with your synchronized steps.

IF YOU ANSWERED MOSTLY BS: You are a bit of a punk rocker. Your love of fast, hard-edged music with defiant, often political lyrics should go down a storm.

IF YOU ANSWERED MOSTLY CS: You could try starting a rap band. Rappers speak rather than sing lyrics to backing music that has a fast, strong beat. Rappers talk about a range of subjects, from problems young people face, to love and money.

IF YOU ANSWERED MOSTLY DS: You were born to rock. You will have the crowd roaring for more of your loud, wild music with its strong, powerful beats and driving rhythms.

Of course, you don't have to stick to one style. There are many other genres of music, from folk to funk. You might like to try different types, a mix of several, or even come up with your own unique sound. Whatever you choose – get out there and make some noise!

GLOSSARY

acoustic when an instrument's sound is not made louder (amplified) by an electronic device

amplifier electronic device that makes sounds louder

ballad slow, sentimental or romantic song

bow long, partly curved rod with horsehair stretched along its length, used for playing the violin and some other stringed instruments

chord two or more notes (or pitches) played together

expenses money it costs to do something, such as travel

harmony combination of musical notes played at the same time to produce chords and chord progressions that sound good; also means being in agreement

idiosyncratic unique feature or style of a person or group

improvise make it up as you go along

jazz style of music with strong but often irregular rhythm that is partly composed and partly made up

lyrics words of a song

melody main tune of a song

metronome device that produces regular ticks to help musicians play in time

mouthpiece part of an instrument which is blown into to play it

open mic event where anyone can sign up to perform

pickup device on a musical instrument that converts sound vibrations into electrical signals for amplification

pitch musical note caused by sound waves vibrating at a particular speed

plectrum small, thin piece of metal or plastic used to pluck a stringed instrument

pluck to pull and release a tight string so it vibrates

recording studio place where music is recorded and mixed

reed thin strip of material, such as bamboo, that vibrates when blown to make a sound

reggae slow-tempo, rhythmic style that originated in Jamaica

rhythm strong, regular, repeated pattern of sound

riff several notes strung together, a recognizable but short part of a rock song – the opening notes of a song that everyone recognizes, for instance

roadie person who sets up the equipment for every show and takes it all down again after the show

rock and roll style of loud popular music featuring several electric guitars

rock opera musical stage show of a story told with rock, rather than classical, music

scale arrangement of notes in ascending or descending order of pitch

sensor device that detects and converts a physical presence into a signal which can be read by a machine

sound waves moving pulses of air we hear as sounds

soundproof to stop sound waves getting in or out of a place

symbol thing that represents or stands for something else, such as a small picture, a mark or a sign

venue place where a show or gig takes place

vibrate move back and forth at a particular speed

FIND OUT MORE

If you are interested in forming a band, you can find lots more advice on the internet, and in the books and DVDs listed here.

To get advice about which musical instrument to choose, visit music shops where you can speak to experts who can advise you on what to get, prices and let you try the instruments right there. You will learn so much from chatting to enthusiasts in a shop. Good music shops also usually have notice boards with lists of local music tutors and local music events, or even second-hand instruments for sale.

To learn more about how bands made it, you could find local musicians to interview for a blog or school magazine. Ask them about how they formed a band and for any tips they have on making bands work.

Even if you have decided which style of music you want to play, it is worth exploring other genres too and seeing what other styles of bands play. This might also inspire you to try new things with your band. You can listen to music on the internet on websites such as Spotify. You can also ask the staff at your local record shop to recommend and play you samples of other bands.

Books

I'm Good At Music What Job Can I Get?, Richard Spilsbury (Wayland, 2013)

Pianos and Keyboards (and other titles in the How The World Makes Music series), Anita Ganeri (Franklin Watts, 2011)

Start a Band! (Find Your Talent), Matt Anniss (Franklin Watts, 2012)

Websites

academyofmusic.ac.uk/southampton
This website includes a step-by-step guide to forming a band.

www.bbc.co.uk/blast/211786
On this website, Yolanda Brown, a saxophonist, offers suggestions on how to choose a musical instrument to suit you.

www.gmarts.org
On this website, you will find tips and more from a musician who has been in a band.

iml.jou.ufl.edu/projects/Fall08/PowellW
This website looks at what other bands do to become successful.

DVDs

School of Rock (2004), Certificate PG
Comedy starring Jack Black, about a guitarist who gets kicked out of a band. He gets a job as a supply teacher and immediately starts turning his class into a blistering rock and roll troupe that can crush his former band at an upcoming competition.

Rock School: The Complete First Series (2005)
Gene Simmons (of the band Kiss) takes on a group of die-hard classical music fans from the super-posh Christ's Hospital school. His plan? To turn them into "Little Rock Gods".

Place to visit

The British Music Experience
www.britishmusicexperience.com
This is a museum of popular music, located at the O2 in London. Using cutting edge audio-visual technology, visitors can trace historic and era-defining moments through 60 years of music history.

Index